She Sings to the Wind

Casmira Lorien

BookLeaf Publishing

Presentation by *BookLeaf Publishing*

Web: www.bookleafpub.com

E-mail: info@bookleafpub.com

ISBN: 9789357613934

First edition 2022

To Aurelia, who makes me want to use my voice.

Sunny Side Up

The perfect sphere
Of yellow sun
Just radiates
In its perfection

A wry smug smile
A gentle nod
I breathe it in
Filled with affection

I've nailed this art
I've got control
And won't you know
That I'm incredible

Ignore the side
The underneath
That's charred and burned
And quite inedible

Coffee and Tea

The difference is -

That unrestrained debauchery.
An intense and vibrant
twang of bitterness,
whose charge sends sirens wailing
in paroxysms of the skin
and grabs at the morning with
both fists.

And the tepid, ghostly pale
of a taste I have to search for.
A firm white hand.
Pinky up.
Voices down.

Kennilworth McDuff

was,
frankly,
a ridiculous man.

Born upside down,
his poor mother shrieked
when they laid him in her arms,
he, perfectly still and staring,
with a heart beating,
on the outside of his chest.

Kennilworth did everything
a little bit backward;
confounding, and confronting.
For example:
he would wake up and put
his pyjamas on;
made tea- milk BEFORE the bag
and on a perfectly sunny day
would arrive at his desk
soaked and shivering
smiling ear to ear
as he went about
typing with his toes.

But worst- that heart
that pulsates with
veiny, wet rhythm
in a way that reminded you
it could *stop* at any time.
So unprotected.
People would cry:
'Kenni, look
The dents! The debris!
You ought to find a jar…
or perhaps
a screen protector?
I dropped my phone
on the kitchen floor,
and not a scratch!

But Kennilworth wept-
far from agreement,
but because he'd stopped
to notice a teacup china pattern
and become enthralled.
Of course, he fell madly
for shoes and ships,
for silver trails of snails
on cabbage leaves,
and the cake crumbs that
dusted the space bar.
He held funerals for the flies
who perished on windowsills,

and floods of tears
cascaded at the concept of cheese.
Forget an art gallery
or a museum.

Kenni couldn't keep a job, nor friend,
nor love for long.
The drumming of his chest
would often
drown out conversation,
and the poor man could not
tear away from 'those eyes'
not for one second,
in case they disappeared
and he couldn't remember them right.

Eventually, his heart began
to shrink.
It was noticed,
and concern (fear of mortality)
rippled through the office,
when the 'boom boom boom'
because a 'patter patter squeak'.

"Have you tried a gym, old mate?
Build that muscle up -
make it strong, like my biceps?"
But Kennilworth looked tired
And his heart puffed a cloud of dust.

And finally,
One sunny day
He had a skin attack
and died.
The mortician
dusted cobwebs
from the ventricles
and his grave read:
Man, with no armour
Loved unrestrained
and helplessly.

The Cloud and the Island

An island
Sat alone
And lonely
In the vast
And open space
Of a blue that
Stretched on
Endlessly.

> he first noticed cloud
> whose skin looked
> like cotton wool and
> shined so full of sunbeams
> as they glided,
> glitterly

through her.

And she noticed him
The way he sprouted
Life from his fingertips
The calm way he
Observed the tides
And sprinkled tiny
Empty spots with
Every kind of flower.

> when she came down
> her skin was wet
> and cold –
> not quite the eiderdown
> she looked.

And he would stand
So. Still.
While   she   scattered
Sometimes stormed.
He couldn't help
But long for
Empty skies.

        and she would often
          look to space
        and wonder, could
      she turn to air? be the
      colour between stars?
        'higher –
           take me higher!'

But rain
Had made
His flowers grow
And he would see
Her form the shapes
Of ships and sheep
And love her
In her flux
Her fog.

        and she would tremble
      at the sight of flowers –
        they really
      much more beautiful
        than stars.

That last fight, from the perspective of the kitchen knife:

I dangled dangerously close
to your skin, shaking, over the sink.
I tried to tell you that I understood,
It felt like you were dying.
But you weren't
And you didn't have to.

You couldn't hear me of course.
Too much yelling
And noise in general-
The reverberation of all that guilt
And the not understanding how anything
Had happened this way.
You who had always been so. sure.

There was a hurt there
That rattled the wallpaper
Made the chrysanthemums cry.

He stood there half-pleading
Half-numb
Willing you to just step back.

Slow down.
Give him more time
To decide the ending.
But you stared down at me as though
Just noticing I was there
And your rasping suddenly felt
Vibrant.

It wasn't an ending you wanted.

A wind blew through you.
Stood you up a little taller.
And I fell, the twang of my blade
Rang with a finality and I caught my breath-

No blood drawn tonight.

The objects of your life,
Sang sadly, sang softly.
A ring left beside me,
On the counter, in the cold.

The Bird

A bird- black and white,
Flew- SMACK- into the window,
Like a gun shot,
Which, while on a phone call,
Caused an almighty screech
To leap from everyone.
The bird lay motionless,
And we stood together
Holding hands,
Contemplating the next step.
Feeling sick.

Two people- who have had their lives
Stripped bare,
But filled with the knowledge
That soon they'll be in charge
Of keeping, something they'd die for,
Alive.
And this bird lies,
Like a spectre of death,
Reminding them of
The danger of windows.

Later,
They will reach the cot
In the early morning,
Cursing your name,
(But holding you tight all the same),
Breathing the fragility of your
Fingers in the moonlight,
And willing tomorrow holds
No surprises
That whip through
Like a gun shot.

The crumpled bird
Dazedly held
The giants in his vision,
Momentarily mourning him.
He was having a bad day,
But he had met windows before,
And decided it was no reason
Not to fly.

Aurelia

Part I

When I first saw you
You were bright pixels splashed
Shining through a darkness-
A whole galaxy that
Swirled beyond my reach
And, suddenly afraid
Of being too small,
I cried.
You've held me, since
With ghost fingers and
Opalescent eyes, while my breath
Falls through to form an atmosphere
That changes constellations into
Heartbeats, beating double.

One night, long ago, we lay
Frost eating our toes
But lovesick,
Staring at the stars
And when he held my hand
I thought I saw your face.

Part II

You are the music that has been
playing in my head,
though the lyrics have always been
changing.
Sometimes forming pebbles that
skim across my stomach.
Sometimes whispering like
smoke on a breeze.
Sometimes existing as a gentle hum that
relaxes fists,
outstretches arms,
pours sunsets outside windows and
expands summer days into infinity.
Sometimes they're mournful,
painting premonitions of pain that my skin
can't stretch around for you.
Inevitably there's a bridge that sings to
all the lives I didn't live.
But the chorus reminds me that,
measure by measure,
you have always been my song.

A Boring Love Poem

Our knees touched,
And we laughed a lot.
We gave each other piggy backs,
While eating crepes,
Which felt like decadence.
A friendship based on
Never wanting to be without
The other.
Enjoying grocery shopping
For the first time.
Watching rockets launch;
The muppets on loop.

You could be in the depths of fury,
And I could hold you and feel
Each little muscle let go,
Submit,
Head on my shoulder.
We're happy here.

*

We lie side by side
and drive side by side
And lounge side by side,
With not much to say.
Our nakedness has become
Normal.
We know each freckle,
We've traced each line.

I read books and you mow the lawn.
You sit and sigh and sit,
As I try things on.

I whip through the house
Like a hurricane,
You follow me with a dustpan.

Knowing you're in the next room.
Missing you when you're downstairs.

We upended our homes,
Sacrificed everything,
For our 'humming-dishwasher' lives.
For finding words in number plates.
For holding hands during the movie.

"I love you" becomes recited,
But it lives in the crinkles
Of our eyes.

Straying

He wasn't bad,
The Wolf.
Those dinner dish eyes
Were blue as midnight.
Soft brown hair,
I could curl my fingers through.
Granny's flowers
Strewn across the forest floor.
We laid the cape over us.
I held him against me.

She found us.

You see,
he taught me things
I couldn't learn
on that
narrow
path.

So, they filled him with stones,
And filled me with lies.
Painted me red.

Lepidopterology

Love died
when it became the goal.
I used to breathe it in:
  Invisible
Before I stuck it to my chest,
like a butterfly in a museum.
'Look at this pretty thing I won!'

With a pin in my heart,
I bled out.

Shiver

You stand there
with a smile that cracks
like ribs,
secretly pawing at the
flesh that makes you
three dimensional,
and grieving.

Where you used to radiate-
now you shiver,
a hollow orchestra
drowns out all other music,
rumbles in a
constant background hum,
ignores the exhaustion.

You, sharpened
in hospital whites,
dying to break from
the too-tiny cage,
that stays invisible to
dumbfounded doctors,
drawing blood and tut-tutting.
You waste their time.
Your hair snaps

When mamma
pulls you in,
you bury your head
in her softness,
and dream of
your body as a
warm pillow.

The Coat Hanger and the Mirror

You make everything seem bigger somehow
The world is so much wider now you're in it
And I can feel myself expanding
You locate my curves, celebrate my edges
A wiry frame built for toughness
And you love the way clothes
Hang off me
Nothing else comes close
The kiss of your light in the morning
Your gut punch in the evening
The way you glitter at the edges
Make me shimmer
Make me cry
I know I'll live in front of you forever
Leaving claw marks
On the glass

On The Roof

One foot in front of the other
hovering between
the air and
the pit of impossibility,
that throws a rope around your heart
and tugs.

There beneath a sky scattered with firelight, is
the
impending suffocation
and the feeling that your back might just sprout
wings

There's a soaring that touches you sometimes,
but it slips silkily through your fingers
and the tiny taste is agony.

You wobble,
knowing that you will be left
like a cracked shell,
swept up by street cleaners
and bleached away.

But this space is the one that says
I am one step away
from that life in the sky,
and maybe.
Just maybe.

Dead Corridors

Punctuated by reaching
You had a hypnotic sway
And a gentle whisper that
Flew through me like a
breeze.

The further up I climbed the more
You dotted the horizon
With a haunted twisting
That agonised the sky
Because we left such spaces
Between you
That your networks pulsed
Then rotted
A series of dead corridors
Telling stories we all needed
To no one but the ground

To the friend I lost in high school:

It was…
pitter patter feet,
then that nourishing embrace,
(the first that ever needed me
before I needed it).

You had those glitter eyes,
and a speed at which you cared,
that made me feel
we were the only ones
who'd considered trees,
or refugees,
or dying.

God. The energy that
threaded you together
(but voltage meeting fabric -
that is how the fires start)

Maybe I loved you?
I certainly spoke of you
on kitchen floors
(wooden spoon hanging from my mouth)
for hours, to my mother

Maybe I could see you,
and it froze me to the ground.
You could leave me
shivering,
and how could I begin?

Maybe I am you,
and it scares me half to death.
Your shadow
sitting on my shoulders,
and a smile
that sings to the wind.

In the Light of Day

This week
we ground our teeth
to dust, imagining
the tiny boxes
for the tiny dead
in Ukraine.

Breastfeeding mothers,
with blood trickling into their
ears, stare at the film crew
with a defeated nonchalance,
getting on with the job
of raising us all
from our graves.

And in the fields of debris
where a city
lays, smouldering
moulders a thumb that someone once
kissed
      crying
'this is the most –
beautiful thumb I've ever seen
the most
beautiful'

I often imagine how she'd look
at me, with love
laced with betrayal
as we yell at her to 'duck'
and she, with hands open
ready to catch
whatever falls from the sky
starts quacking.

Every shining fragile hand,
a mortal.
Every war a sharp focus.
Every wish carried into the wind and
replaced with a narrative.

Today we watched a golden braided/
honey voice cut through
a bomb shelter.
Let the storm rage on. We sang along.
Swallowed.
Took our children
outside.

An Act of War

"Things like that don't happen here"
but comfort and be comforted
in the eerie quiet
of trying to comprehend icons
burning to the ground.

Make eye contact
as sidewalks become
a chorus
"did you know someone?"

The papers
sprouting from the sky
with urgent trauma.
      It would be ungrateful to panic.

Outdoor stops with perfect views;
I eyed them every morning.
To experience the relief of laughter.
Rising to the challenge of
justifying joy
within the horror stench
in the air.

Jet fuel.

I had
Never
Will
Never
Know
Racist
Or
Religious
Violence

I can sit outside myself
                    so safe.

'Never Forget' means
look how we forget those
who need us
every day.

Offstage

When I wipe my face clean
And sit down as myself
I notice
My skin stretched
so tight
across stories
that weren't mine
It became
Translucent

Sometimes when the light hits
just right
There's a glint.
You could
Catch my eye – in its

Ornamental nothingness

A shapeshifter
Exists like the wind
She's wild and she rages
But she holds up her hand
And sees only the leaves
That dance inside her

My Father

My father without a father
    Began,
Ruler down his back.
Straight desks and straight spines,
Reciting lines,
A long thin 'smack',
Will turn these boys to men.
      He chose
Not to swallow tears.
Sought to make straight edges round,
Fists towards the ground,
And met his fears,
He knows that's how he grows.

My father without a father,
   He saw
Every shade of grey,
Spent a life of watching, hearing
Voices of the disappearing,
Stood with them in their dismay,
Grew the silence to a roar.
     And wise
Learned that stories shared,
 Connected us in human grief,
An open chest can find relief,
In knowing we were scared,
Could see with different eyes.

My father without a father,
    Books on shelves,
Gently opened every door,
And friends with floor and with the sky,
Would let us fall and help us fly,
We'd search and we'd explore,
And turn into ourselves.
    Undone,
With bittersweet delight,
These children he'd keep warm and hold,
Could not protect, but gently mould,
They'd radiate with light,
Because he was the sun.

the gentle sex

I make hurricanes
With whispers
And delight
The twists and turns

I cause rumbles inside
Mountains
As the forest beneath
Burns

I am the shudder
Under foot
The wind that whines
And whips

I push
And pull the tides
And in my free time
I sink ships

Modern Love

Ambitious and radical
-　　　　there's avocado.

It's a fruit. It's seasonal.
So bolt it to a menu.

A textured, tasty green paste-
the focus is on breakfast
in a caved, brutal concrete.

Signalled boldly, this beasts bursts
out of the pack!

Delights in the modern.

A room out back burbles contemporary
　　　　and sold- sets them simmering.

It's a big, filling, 'feed me' dish.

Dietary requirements:
gluten free. no animal products.
coffee grounds composted. and generated
with Instagram in mind.